and Activity

Use a Map

Jill is playing hide-and-seek. Read about where she looks for her friends. Then look at that place on the map. Next draw a line to the picture that answers each question.

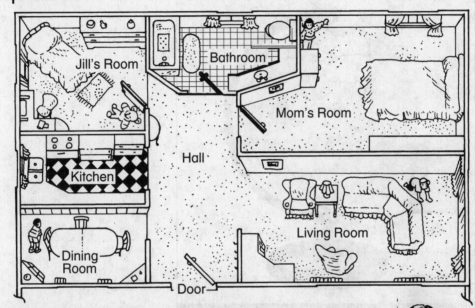

1. Jill looks in the dining room. Look at the map. Who is in the dining room?

2. Jill looks in the room across the hall from the dining room. Who is in that room?

3. Jill looks in the room next to the living room. Who is there?

4. Jill takes her friends to her room. Circle Jill's room on the map.

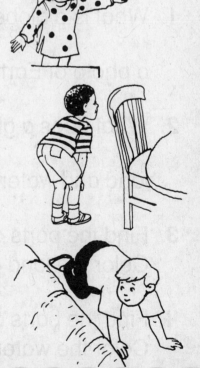

Use a Globe

Look at the globe on this page. Then follow the directions.

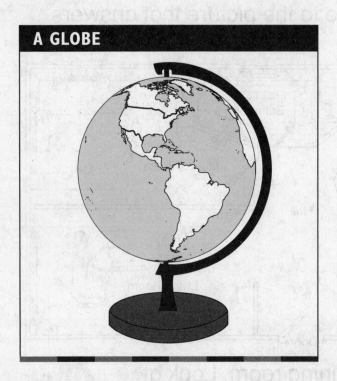

A GLOBE

1. What is a globe? (Circle one)

   a photo of Earth   a model of Earth

2. What does a globe show? (Circle one)

   land and water   people and homes

3. Find the parts of the globe that show land.
   Color the land green.

4. Find the parts of the globe that show water.
   Color the water blue.

Name: _____ Date: _____

My Family

Draw pictures of people in your family. Use the picture frames. Share your drawings with a friend.

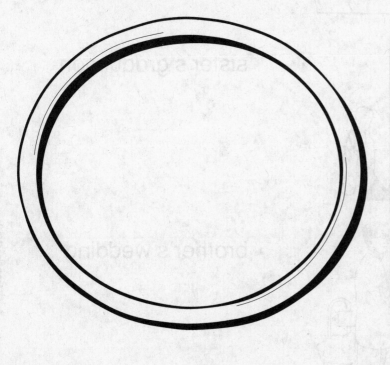

A Family Celebrates

The pictures tell about Chen. Chen is celebrating some special days with his family. Draw a line from each picture to the words that tell about it.

1.

Chen's birthday

2.

Chinese New Year

3.

sister's graduation

4.

brother's wedding

My Neighborhood

Part 1: Draw a picture to show where you live.

Where I live

Part 2: Circle the name of a place in your neighborhood. Draw a picture of it.

library   neighbor's house   firehouse   school

What's the Address?

Mike lives on Elm Street. He is going to visit
some neighbors. Read about where Mike
goes. Circle the answer to each question.

1. Mike is standing in front of his house.
   What is Mike's address?

   12 Elm Street   14 Elm Street

2. Mike walks to 12 Elm Street.
   Who lives at that address?

   Kim   Roberto

3. Next Mike visits Maria.
   What is Maria's address?

   16 Elm Street   18 Elm Street

©Macmillan/McGraw-Hill

Rules at School

Read each rule. Circle the picture that shows children following the rule.

1. Do not talk in the library.

2. Do not run in the hall.

3. Hang up your coat.

4. Wait in line until your turn comes.

People and Places

Practice and Activity

Solve a Problem

Look at the picture. Read the caption under the picture. Then follow the directions.

Debbie has a problem. She does not have a safe place to ride her bike.

1. Help Debbie solve her problem. Which sentence tells the best solution? Put an X next to it.

    _____ Debbie can sell her bike to a friend.

    _____ Mom can take Debbie to the park to ride.

    _____ Debbie can move to a new neighborhood.

2. Draw a picture showing Debbie's solution.

©Macmillan/McGraw-Hill

Using Transportation

The picture shows seven kinds of transportation.
Draw a circle around each kind. Count your circles.
Do you have seven?

Read a Chart

Look at the chart. Read the title to learn what the chart is about. Answer each question.

THINGS WE LIKE TO DO				
	SWIMMING	LISTENING TO STORIES	PAINTING	PLAYING OUTDOORS
Alex	X	X		
Joan	X	X	X	
Ben			X	X

1. Circle the things Alex enjoys.

2. Circle the things Joan enjoys.

3. Circle the thing that both Joan and Ben enjoy.

Looking at Change

Read the stories. Follow the directions.

1. Mary's family travels in a wagon. A horse pulls the wagon. Circle the picture of Mary's family.

2. How does your family get around? Circle one picture.

3. Jack's mother cooks dinner. She uses an open fire. Circle the picture of Jack's mother.

4. How does your family cook dinner? Circle one picture.

©Macmillan/McGraw-Hill

Name: _____   Date: _____

Kenya Is in Africa

Look at the map. Follow the directions.

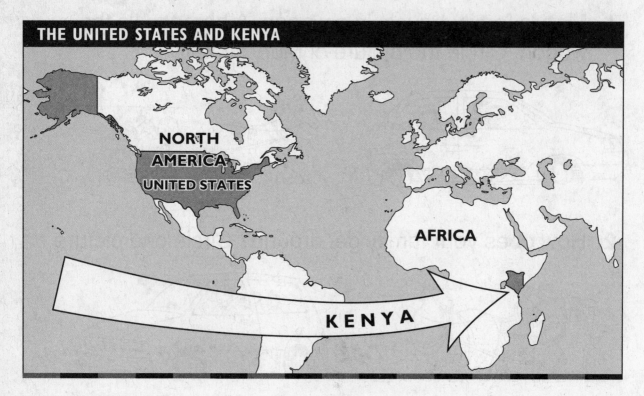

THE UNITED STATES AND KENYA

NORTH AMERICA
UNITED STATES

AFRICA

K E N Y A

1. Find the United States on the map.
   Circle it in red.

2. Find Africa on the map. Africa is a continent.
   Color it yellow.

3. Look at Africa. Find the country of Kenya outlined in black. Write the word Kenya on the line.

_____

- -

_____

Using New Words

Draw a line from each word to the picture it goes with.

1. family

2. home

3. neighborhood

4. address

5. holiday

6. transportation

We Live in Communities

Rose has friends in different communities.
Color each path that leads to a community.

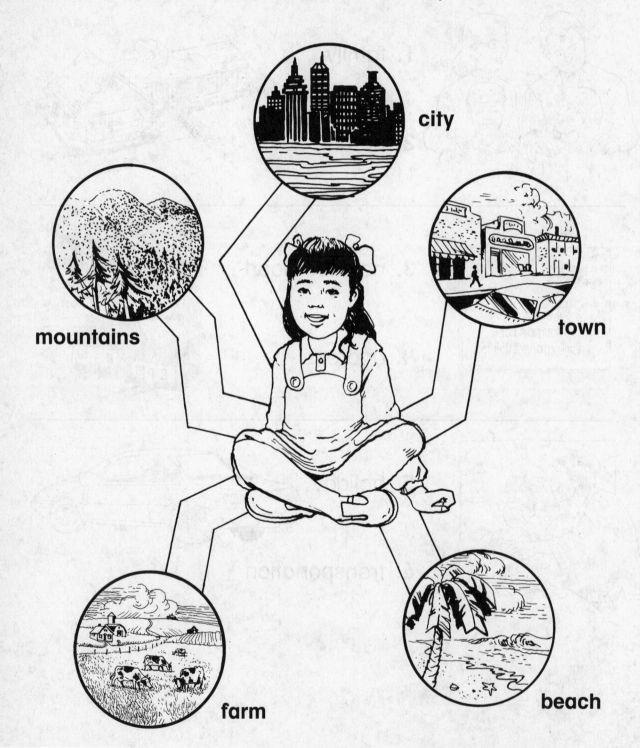

city

mountains

town

farm

beach

Name: _____   Date: _____

Using Pictures and Maps

The model shows how Tim's community looks from an airplane. Color the picture. Then answer the question.

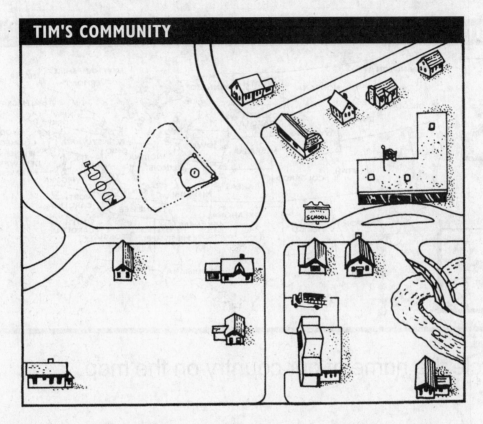

TIM'S COMMUNITY

Which map shows Tim's community? (Circle one)

Map A

Map B

©Macmillan/McGraw-Hill

Name: _____   Date: _____

Our Country

Look at the map of our country. Then finish the activity.

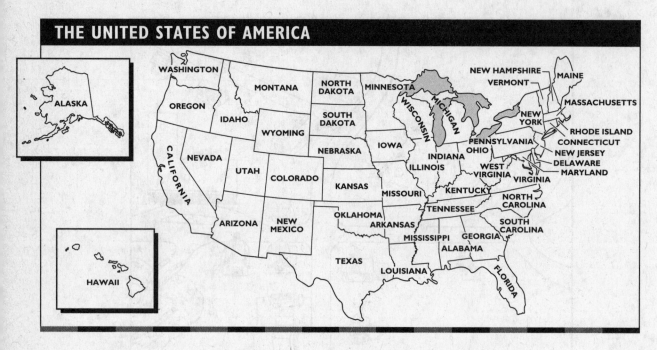

THE UNITED STATES OF AMERICA

1. Circle the name of our country on the map.

2. What is the name of your state?

   _____

   -

   _____

3. Find your state on the map.
   Color it red.

4. How many states does our country have?
   (Circle one)

          30   40   50

Sorting Pictures into Groups

The word in each section below names a group.
Circle the pictures that belong in each group.

Transportation

Toys

Work

Our Continent

Look at the map. Follow the directions.

NORTH AMERICA

NORTH

WEST

EAST

PACIFIC OCEAN

CANADA

UNITED STATES

ATLANTIC OCEAN

MEXICO

SOUTH

1. Find the United States on the map.
   Color it blue.

2. To which continent does the United States belong?
   (Circle one)

   South America   North America

3. Find the country that is our neighbor to the north.
   Color it green.

4. Find the country that is our neighbor to the south.
   Color it red.

Looking at Land and Water

Sam's family went on a vacation. Here are some pictures they took. Write the word from the box that tells about each picture.

plain   hills   lake   ocean   river   mountains

1.

_____

- - - - - - - - - - - - - -

_____

2.

_____

- - - - - - - - - - - - - -

_____

3.

_____

- - - - - - - - - - - - - -

_____

4.

_____

- - - - - - - - - - - - - -

_____

5.

_____

- - - - - - - - - - - - - -

_____

6.

_____

- - - - - - - - - - - - - -

_____

Name: _____   Date: _____

Use a Map Key

Look at the map key. Find the symbols on the map.
Then circle the answer to each question.

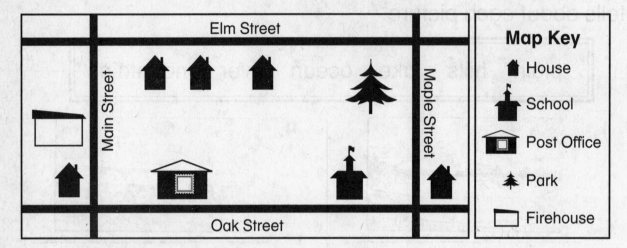

1. Which symbol stands for a park?

2. Which symbol stands for a school?

3. How many houses does the map show?

   1   2   3   4   5

4. On which street is the school?

   Elm Street   Oak Street   Maple Street

5. Find the firehouse on the map.
   Color the firehouse red.

Unit 2 · pp. 90–91

What Is the Weather?

Draw a line from each picture to the word or words that tell about it.

1.  sunny

snowy

2. rainy

3. hot

4. windy

cold

Think about the weather where you live. What is the weather today? Write your answer below.

_____

_ _

_____

Our Natural Resources

How can you help take care of Earth's natural resources? Color each path that leads to a way.

Ways to Care for Natural Resources

Throw garbage on the ground.

Throw garbage in the trash can.

Use things over and over.

Take care of our animals.

Clean up your park.

©Macmillan/McGraw-Hill

Where is Switzerland?

Look at the map. Then follow the directions.

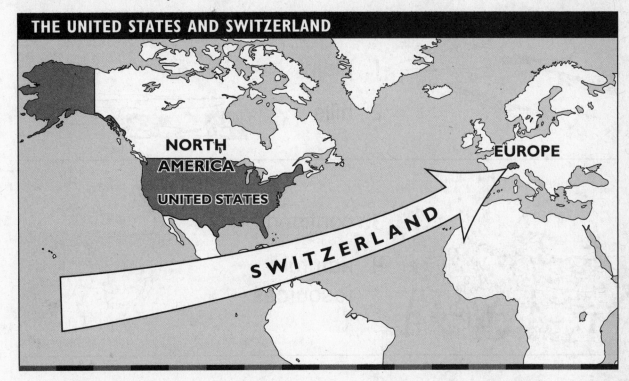

THE UNITED STATES AND SWITZERLAND

NORTH AMERICA

UNITED STATES

EUROPE

SWITZERLAND

I. Find the United States on the map. Circle it in red.

2. Find Switzerland on the map. Where is Switzerland? (Circle one)
North America
Europe

3. What is Switzerland? (Circle one)
a country
a continent

4. Write the word Switzerland on the line.

_____

- -

_____

Using New Words

Draw a line to the picture each word tells about.

1. plain

2. hills

3. continent

4. natural resources

5. mountains

6. ocean

7. lake

8. river

9. seasons

10. farm

©Macmillan/McGraw-Hill

People Belong to Groups

Dan belongs to many groups. Read about those groups. Draw a line from each sentence to the picture the sentence tells about.

1. Dan goes on picnics with his family.

2. Dan learns new things with his class.

3. Dan is on a baseball team.

4. Dan flies a kite with his friends.

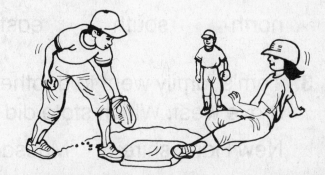

Using Directions

Tom's family visited Vermont. Use the map to answer the questions about their trip. Circle the answer to each question.

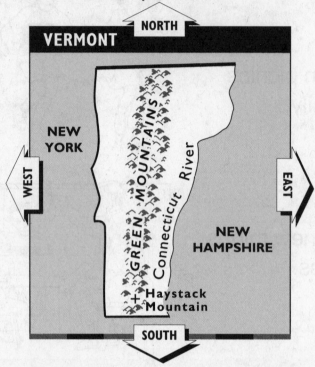

I. Tom's family drove across the Connecticut River. In which part of the state is this river?

north   south   east   west

2. Tom's family visited Haystack Mountain. In which part of the state is this mountain?

north   south   east   west

3. Tom's family went to another state. They drove west. Which state did they go to?

New Hampshire   Massachusetts   New York

Laws Keep People Safe

Each sentence tells a law. Draw a line to the picture that matches the law.

1. Fasten your seatbelt.

2. No swimming.

3. No littering.

4. Stop at the stop sign.

I Am a Leader

Each sentence tells about a leader. Read the stories. Draw a line from each sentence to the picture it matches.

1. I help make your community a safe place.

Firefighter

2. I help you to learn and grow.

The President

3. I am the leader of our country, the United States of America.

Police Officer

4. I protect your community from fire.

Teacher

©Macmillan/McGraw-Hill

Name: _____   Date: _____

Marty's Class Trip

Look at the chart. See what Marty's class voted for.
Then circle the answer to each question.

VOTING ON A CLASS TRIP		
Zoo	X X X X X	5 votes
Park	X X X	3 votes
Pet Fair	X X X X X X X X	8 votes

1. How many children voted to go to the park?

　1　　2　　3　　4　　5　　6　　7　　8

2. For which trip did five children vote?

3. For which trip did the most children vote?

Symbol Riddles

Circle the picture that goes with each riddle.

1. I rang when the United States became a country. I stand for freedom. You can see me in Philadelphia.

2. I stand for hope, freedom, and friendship. You can see me in New York Harbor. I welcome people coming to our country from other places.

3. I am red, white, and blue. I have 13 stripes and 50 stars. Each star stands for one of our 50 states.

4. I am a special bird. You can see me on some of our country's money.

Name: _____   Date: _____

Using a Calendar

Use the calendar to answer the questions.

May						
Sunday	Monday	Tuesday	Wednesday	Thursday	Friday	Saturday
	1	2	3	4	5	6
7	8	9	10	11	12	13
14 Mother's Day	15	16	17	18	19	20
21	22	23	24	25	26	27
28	29 Memorial Day	30	31			

1. Which month does the calendar show? _____

2. How many days are in this month? _____

3. On which day of the week is Memorial Day?

_____

_____

4. Which special day is on May 14?

_____

_____

©Macmillan/McGraw-Hill

A Good Citizen

Read each story. Circle the picture that matches the story.

1. I was a runaway slave. I worked to free African Americans.

Clara Barton

Frederick Douglass

Eleanor Roosevelt

2. I began the Red Cross in America. The Red Cross helps people in need.

Clara Barton

Frederick Douglass

Eleanor Roosevelt

3. I worked to help poor people. I wanted life to be fair for everyone.

Clara Barton

Frederick Douglass

Eleanor Roosevelt

Meet Miko

Miko lives in Japan. You and Miko are alike in many ways. Draw a picture of you next to Miko. Draw a line from the picture to each way you and Miko are alike.

speak Japanese

live in Japan

Miko   **Me**

have friends

have a family

wear special hats to school

go to school

©Macmillan/McGraw-Hill

Using New Words

Draw a line from each word to the picture it goes with.

1. calendar

2. citizen

3. laws

4. vote

5. flag

6. groups

©Macmillan/McGraw-Hill

Name: _____   Date: _____

Needs and Wants

Draw a line from the word to the picture it goes with.

1. need

2. want

3. need

4. want

5. need

6. want

7. need

8. want

©Macmillan/McGraw-Hill

Work People Do

A job is work that people do. Circle the pictures that show people working to help others. Draw a line under the pictures that show people making or growing something.

baker

police officer

farmer

school bus driver

doctor

builder

barber

rug maker

sanitation worker

©Macmillan/McGraw-Hill

Finding Service Workers

The picture shows six service workers. Find the service workers. Then draw a circle around each one. Now color the picture.

Name: _____   Date: _____

Using Picture Graphs

Joey, Liz, and Mark went to the bicycle store. They saw some new bikes. Use the picture graph to answer the questions. Circle the correct answers.

PEOPLE	NUMBER OF BICYCLES EACH PERSON SAW 🚲 = One Bicycle
Joey	🚲 🚲 🚲 🚲
Liz	🚲 🚲 🚲 🚲 🚲 🚲
Mark	🚲 🚲 🚲

I. What does the picture graph show?

the number of bicycles   the number of people
each person saw   who have bicycles

2. How many bicycles did Mark see?

I   2   3   4   5   6

3. Who saw the most bicycles?

Joey   Liz   Mark

Buying Goods

Draw a line from each coin or bill to its name.
Then draw a line from the name of the coin or
bill to the picture that shows the same value.

1.    one dollar

2.   dime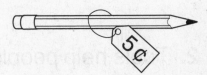

3.    nickel

4.    quarter

Which costs more, the comb or the toy horse?
Write the answer below.

_____

- -

_____

New Tools at Work

Read the sentences. Then use the words from the box to fill in the blanks.

```
tools • job • new • changed • work
```

1. Many people use _____.

2. Tools help people do a better _____.

3. Over the years, tools have _____.

4. Today farmers use _____ tools.

5. Now farmers can do more _____.

Putting Pictures in Order

Look at each group of pictures. Put them in order to tell a story. Draw a line from the number to the picture it goes with.

Kim builds a sandman.

1.

2.

Tony makes an airplane.

1.

2.

3.

Learning About Great Ideas

Amy wants to learn about people who have great ideas. Color each path that shows a person who had a great idea.

Brazilians Make Goods

The map shows three kinds of goods made in Brazil. Find the pictures of goods on the map. Circle the goods with a crayon. Then answer the questions.

1. Which city is the capital of Brazil? (Circle one)

   Brasília   São Paulo

2. Which city makes computers? (Circle one)

   Brasília   São Paulo

Write the word Brazil on the line.

_____

- - - - - - - - - - - - - - - - - - -

_____

Using New Words

Circle the word that goes with the pictures.

1.

wants   needs

2.

HELP CLEAN UP THE PARK

TRASH

volunteer   shelter

3.

FLAKES

service   goods

4.

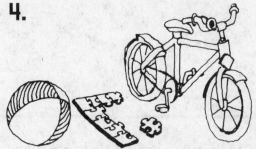

needs   wants

5.

STOP

job   goods

6.

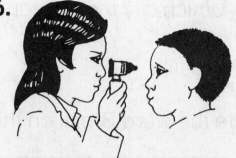

goods   service

The Navajo

Look at the picture. Follow the directions.

1. Find the Navajo houses in the picture. Color them brown.

Write the name for these houses.

_____

_ _ _ _ _ _ _ _ _ _ _

_____

2. Find the Navajo who is making a rug. Circle that person.

3. The Navajo used clay

_____

_ _ _ _ _ _ _ _ _ _

and _____ to

make houses.

4. Circle the word or words that tell about the Navajo people.

buffalo hunters

Native Americans

basketmakers

Using a Time Line

The time line shows what Pam did on her vacation.
Circle the answer to each question.

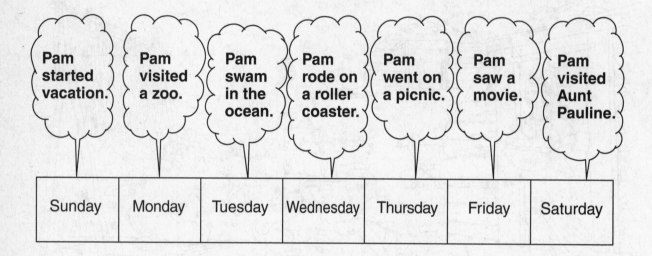

| Sunday | Monday | Tuesday | Wednesday | Thursday | Friday | Saturday |

1. What do the boxes on the time line stand for?

   days   months   years

2. On which day did Pam start her vacation?

   Saturday   Tuesday   Sunday

3. What did Pam do on Monday?

   saw a movie   visited a zoo   went on a picnic

4. When did Pam visit Aunt Pauline?

   Tuesday   Thursday   Saturday

Columbus Sails to America

Look at the map. Follow the directions.

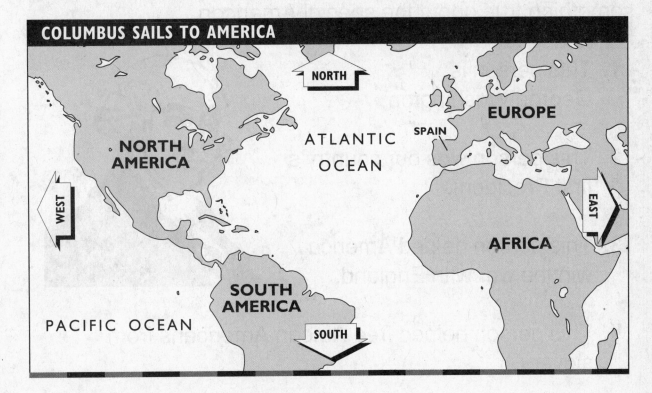

COLUMBUS SAILS TO AMERICA

NORTH

EUROPE

SPAIN

ATLANTIC OCEAN

NORTH AMERICA

WEST

EAST

AFRICA

SOUTH AMERICA

PACIFIC OCEAN

SOUTH

1. Find the country Columbus sailed from.
Color that country red.

2. Find the ocean Columbus sailed across.
Color the ocean blue.

3. Draw a line to show where Columbus's ships
crossed the ocean.

© Macmillan/McGraw-Hill

A Special American

Circle the number of each sentence that says something true about the special American.

1. This person is George Washington.

2. This person was our country's first President.

3. This person helped America win the war with England.

4. This person helped free African Americans from slavery.

5. This person is called the "Father of our Country."

Circle the name of the holiday on which we remember this person.

Thanksgiving   Presidents' Day   Columbus Day

Sacagawea

Read the sentences about Sacagawea. Then answer the questions. Write the number of each sentence next to the words that match it.

1. When did Sacagawea live?

2. To which Native American group did Sacagawea belong?

3. Which two important people did Sacagawea help?

4. What place did the two people want to learn more about?

5. What did Sacagawea show the two people?

6. Which ocean did Sacagawea help find?

_____ Lewis and Clark

_____ trails to take

_____ long ago

_____ Pacific Ocean

_____ Shoshoni Indians

_____ North America

A Special President

Circle the number of each sentence that says something true about the special President.

1. This person is Abraham Lincoln.

2. This person was our country's first President.

3. This person was President during the Civil War.

4. This person helped free African Americans from slavery.

5. This person is called "Honest Abe."

Circle the name of the building that honors Abraham Lincoln.

Lincoln Memorial   Civil War   Honest Abe

Susan B. Anthony

Read the sentences. Then choose a word from the word box to finish the sentences. Put the number of the word on the blank line.

1. women	**2.** vote	
3. right	**4.** fair	
5. worked		

1. Long ago, women were not allowed to

_____

_ _ _ _ _ _ _ _ _

_____ .

2. Susan B. Anthony knew it was not

_____

_ _ _ _ _ _ _ _ _

_____ to keep

women from voting.

_____

_ _ _ _ _ _ _ _ _

3. Many _____

wanted to change the voting laws.

4. Susan B. Anthony and other women

_____

_ _ _ _ _ _ _ _ _

_____ to get

the law changed.

5. After many years of work, women won the

_____

_ _ _ _ _ _ _ _ _

_____ to vote.

Finding the Main Idea

Read each story. Then draw a line under the sentence in the story that tells the main idea.

1. Columbus sailed three ships

   across the ocean. They were

   called the *Niña,* the *Pinta,* and

   the *Santa María.* The ships were

   made of wood. Each ship had

   sails to catch the wind.

2. The Taino welcomed Columbus

   and his men. The Taino gave

   the sailors birds and plants.

   They also gave the sailors

   tomatoes and corn. The sailors

   had never seen these foods before.

©Macmillan/McGraw-Hill

Name: _____   Date: _____

Martin Luther King, Jr.

Follow the directions to complete the activity.
Circle your answers.

1. As a boy, Martin Luther King, Jr., went to a school for black children only. Why?

It was the law.

He lived in Atlanta.

He rode a bus to school.

2. As a man, what did Martin Luther King, Jr., work to change?

Atlanta, Georgia   schools   unfair laws

3. What was Martin Luther King, Jr.'s, dream?

people becoming heros   people working together

4. What did Martin Luther King, Jr.'s, work help do?

close schools in Atlanta, Georgia

end laws that kept people apart

5. How do we remember Martin Luther King, Jr.?

as a marcher   as a hero   as a dreamer

Where is Mexico?

Study the map. Then follow the directions.

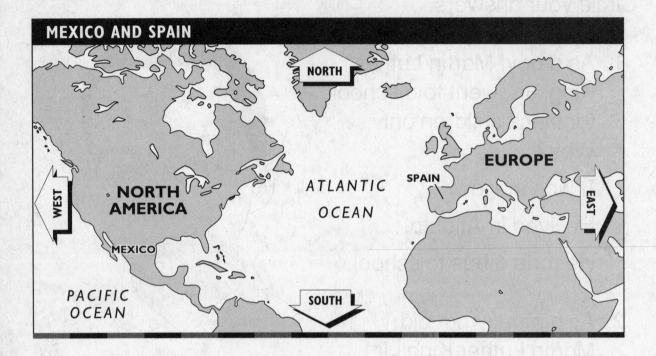

MEXICO AND SPAIN

NORTH

WEST

NORTH AMERICA

MEXICO

ATLANTIC OCEAN

SPAIN

EUROPE

EAST

PACIFIC OCEAN

SOUTH

I. Find Mexico on the map. Circle it in yellow.

2. Find the country that once ruled Mexico. Circle it in orange.

3. Which hero helped free Mexico from Spain? (Circle one)

   Miguel Hidalgo   Abraham Lincoln

4. What does "Viva Mexico!" mean? (Circle one)

   "Long Life!"   "Long Live Mexico!"

New Words and Ideas

Draw a line from each definition to the word it matches.

I.

settlers who came to North America from England

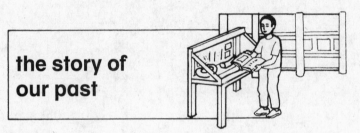

history

2.

the story of our past

Native Americans

3.

the first people to live in America

settlers

4.

a small community

Pilgrims

5.

people who move from one place to live in another place

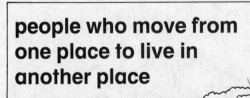

settlement

©Macmillan/McGraw-Hill

Activities

Activity Book

This section gives patterns for use with Unit Projects.

Materials	Unit 1	Unit 2	Unit 3	Unit 4	Unit 5
pencils, crayons, markers, scissors, glue, tape	★	★	★	★	★
drawing and construction paper	★	★	★	★	★
mural paper		★			
oaktag			★		
coat hangers and yarn				★	
yarn and clothespins					★

Ongoing Unit Projects

Make a Family Scrapbook

Draw a picture about your family.
Then cut out the picture.

Make a Geography Mural

Fill in the grid map with pictures of your community.

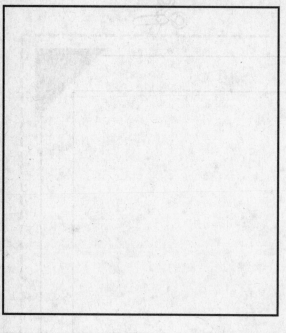

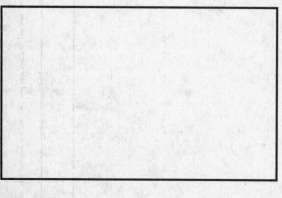

©Macmillan/McGraw-Hill

Make a Jigsaw Puzzle

Fill in the jigsaw puzzle piece. Then cut it out.

People and Places

Practice and Activity

Make a Work Mobile

Complete the sentence and draw a picture in the space below. Cut out your picture.

_____

_ _ _ _ _ _ _ _ _ _ _ _ _ _ _ _ _ _ _

How can we show _____?

©Macmillan/McGraw-Hill

Unit 4: Ongoing Unit Project

Make a History Time Line

Color the arrow.
Then cut it out.

Our Nation's Symbols: American Flag